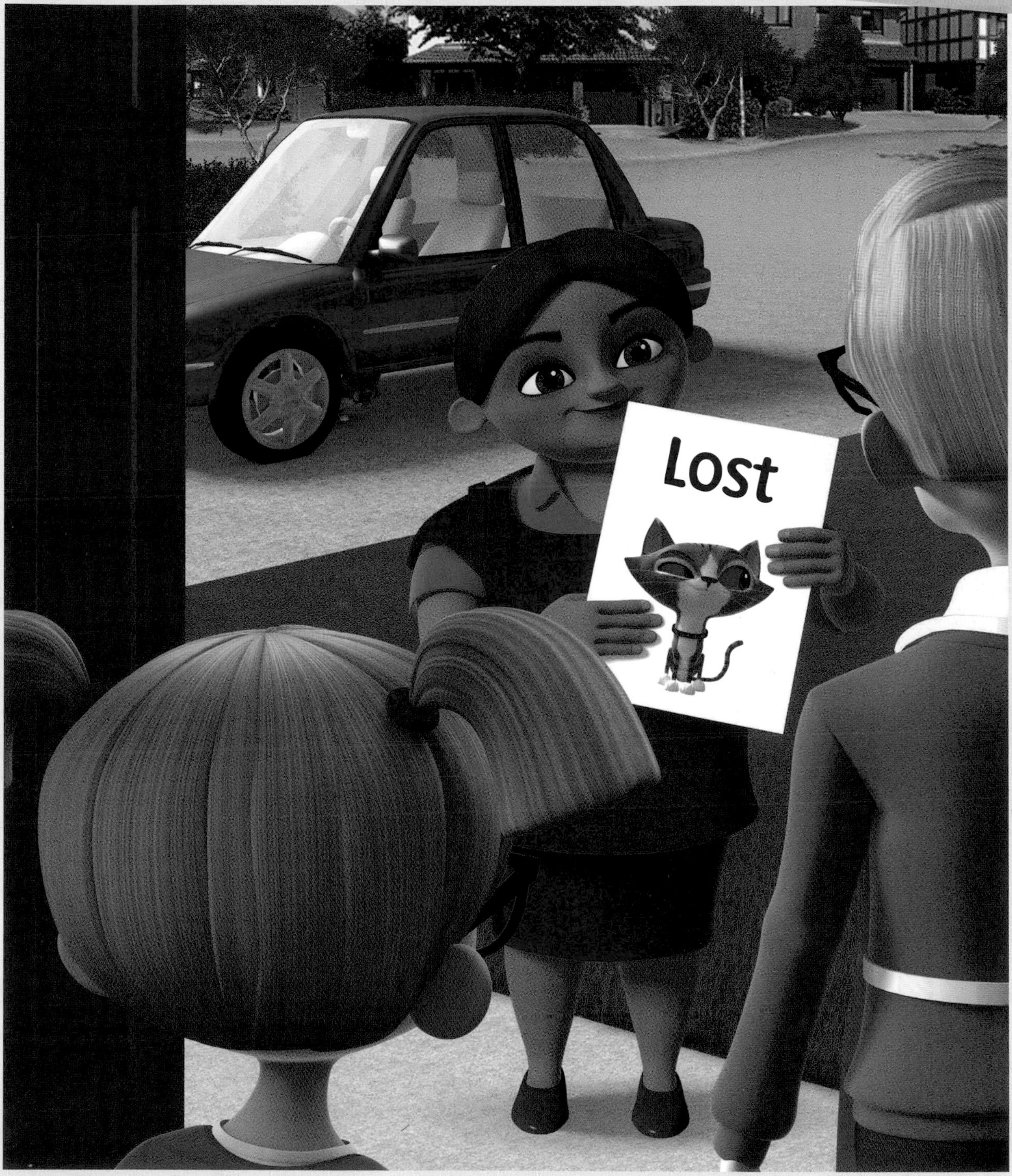
Lost

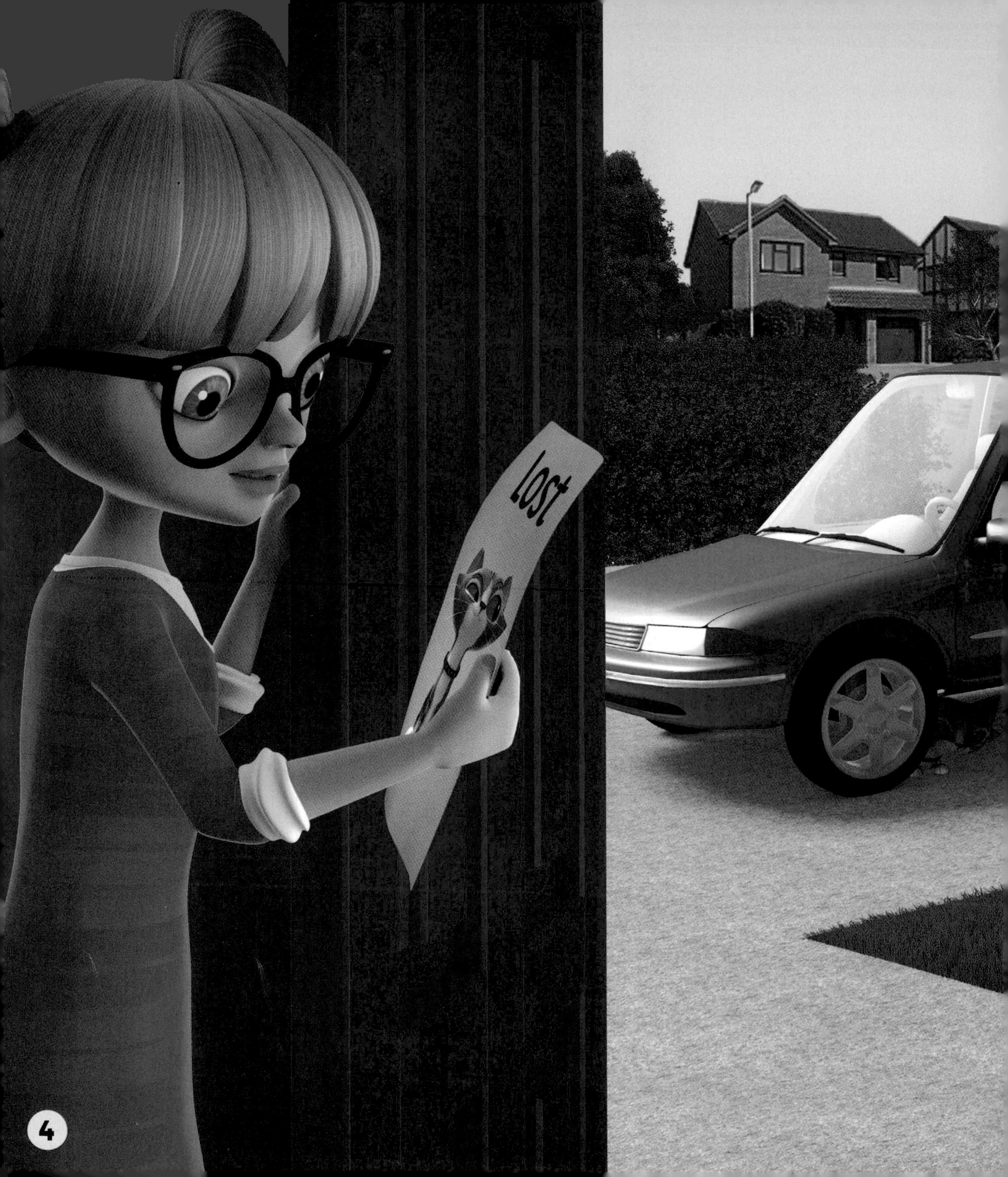
Lost

The Los

C

by

Illustrate

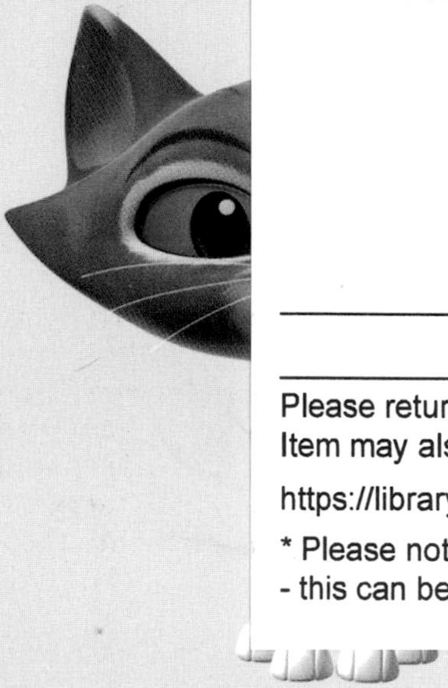

OXFORD
UNIVERSITY PRESS

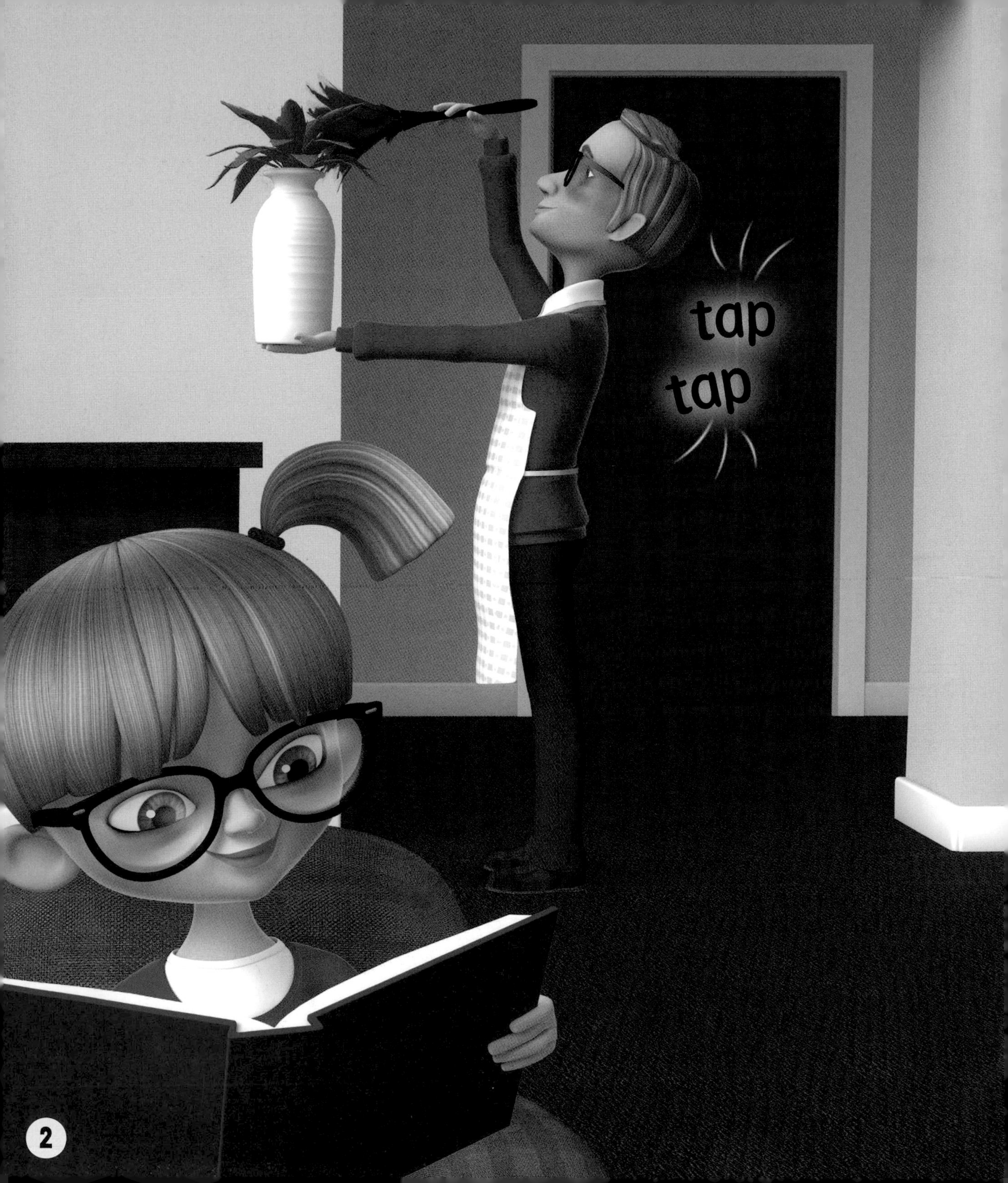
tap
tap

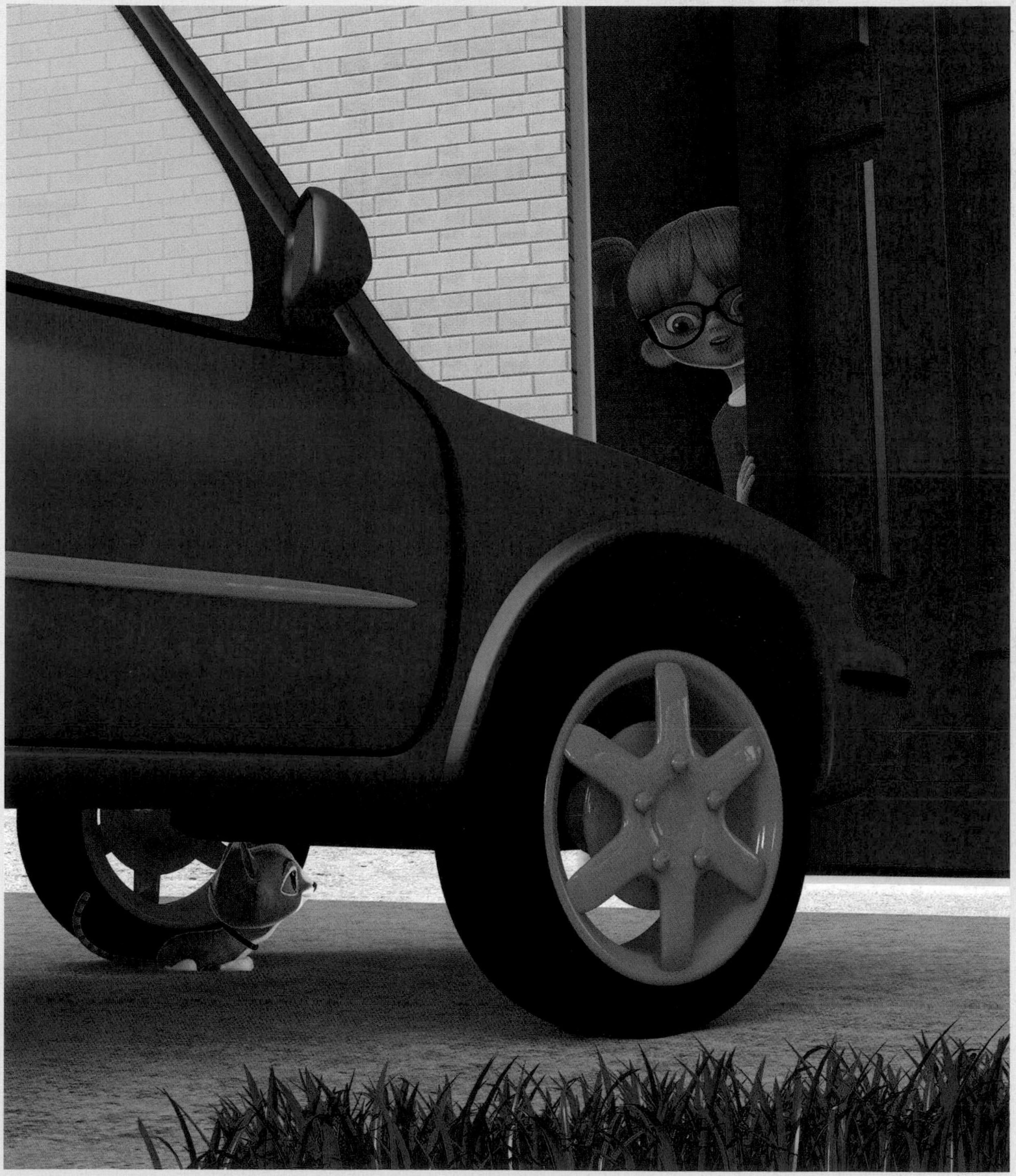

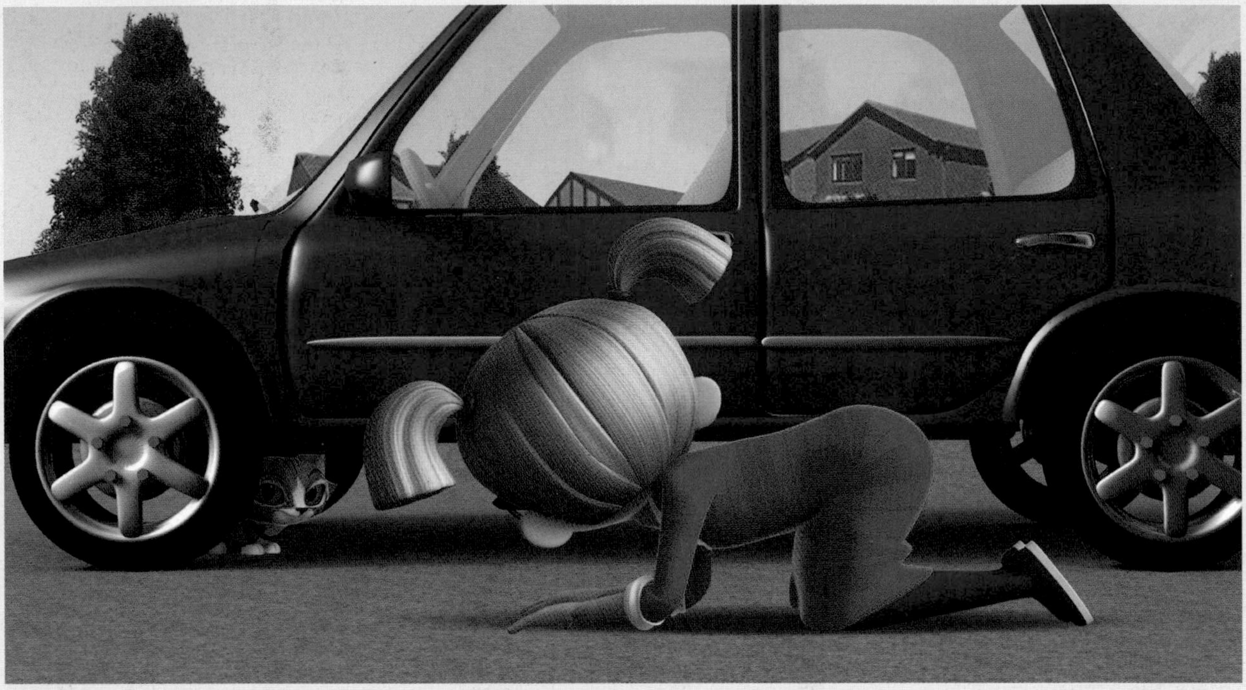

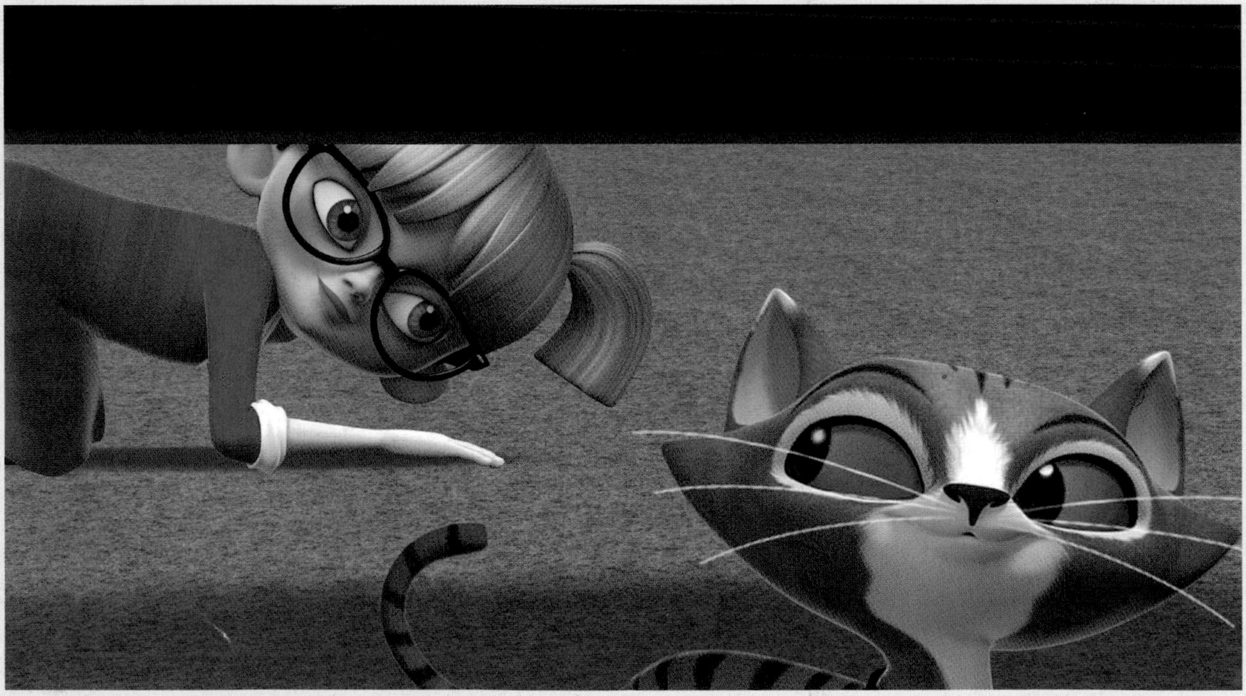

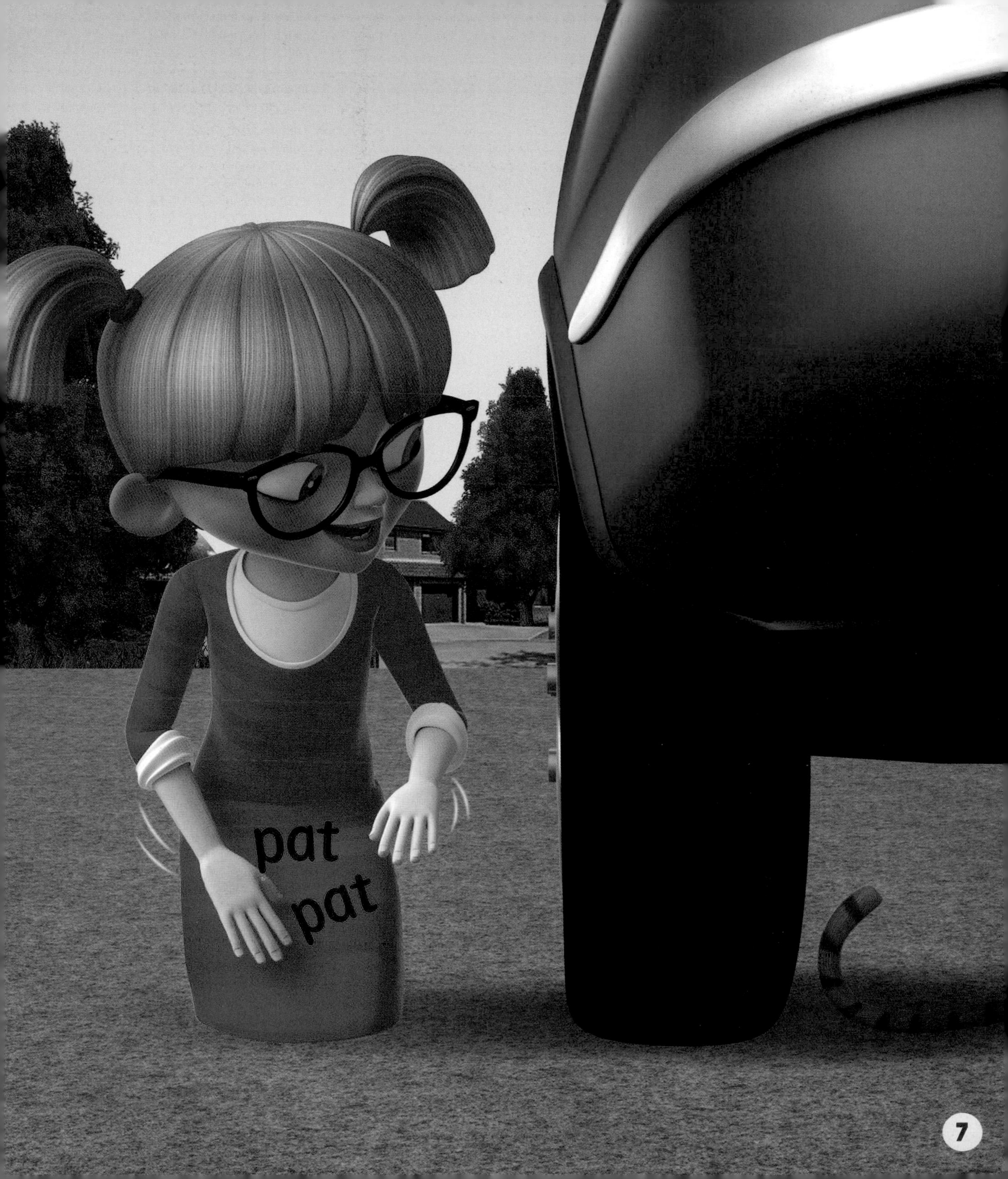
pat
pat

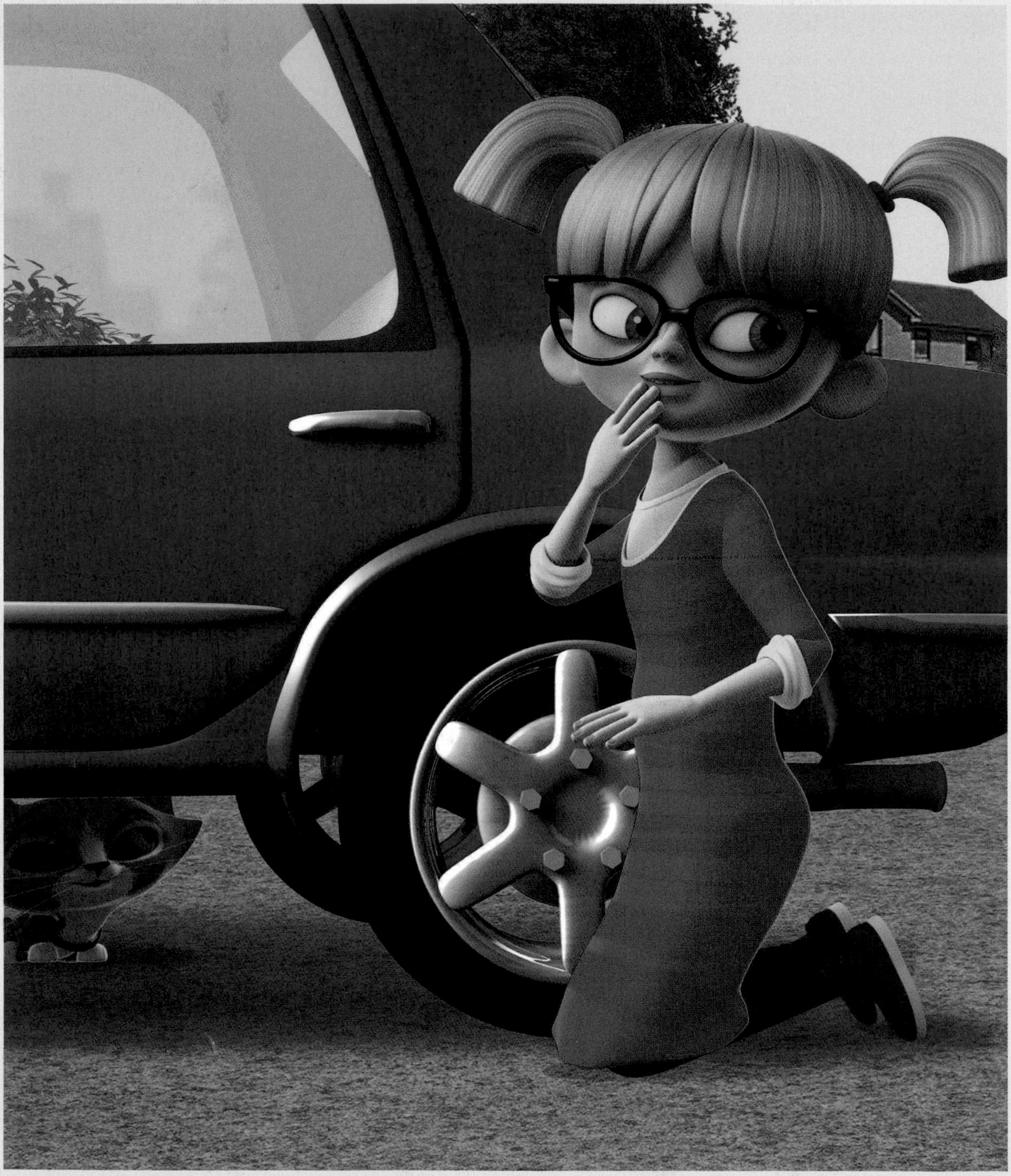

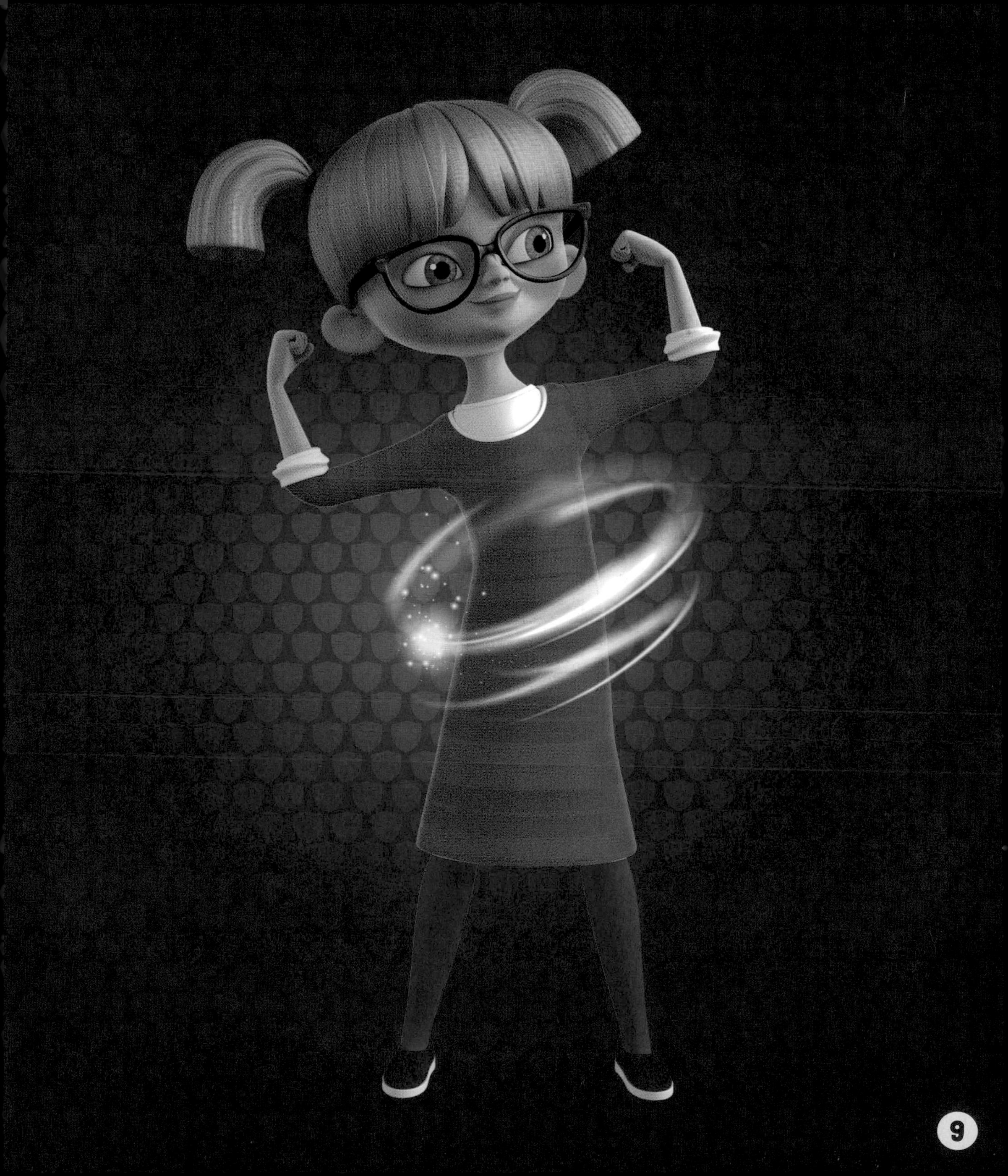

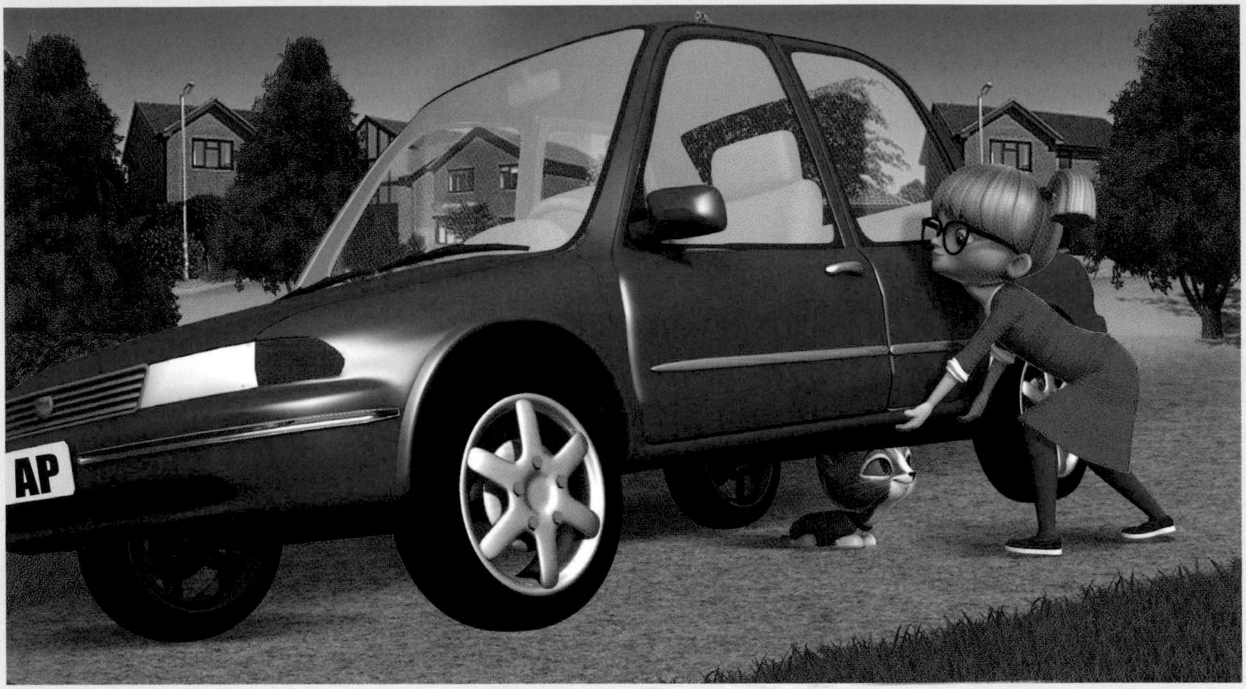
AP

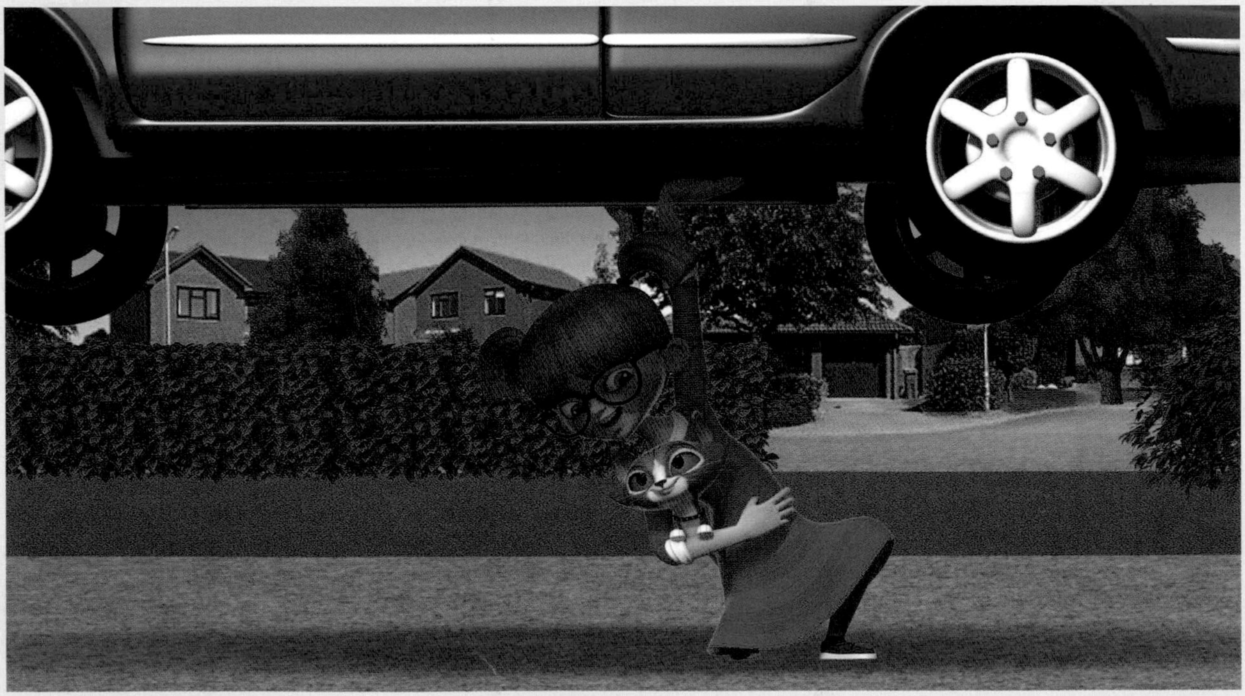

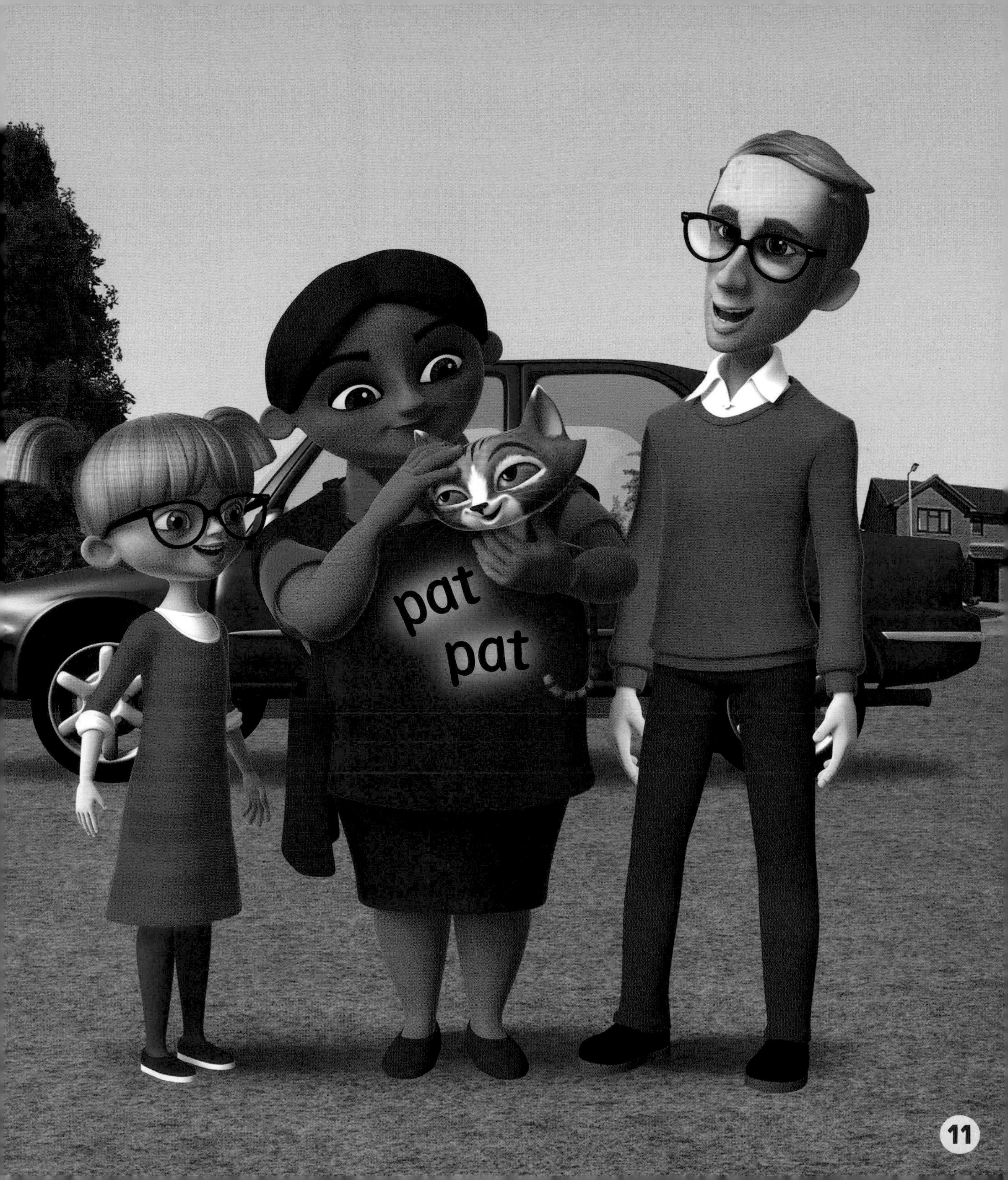
pat
pat

Retell the story ...

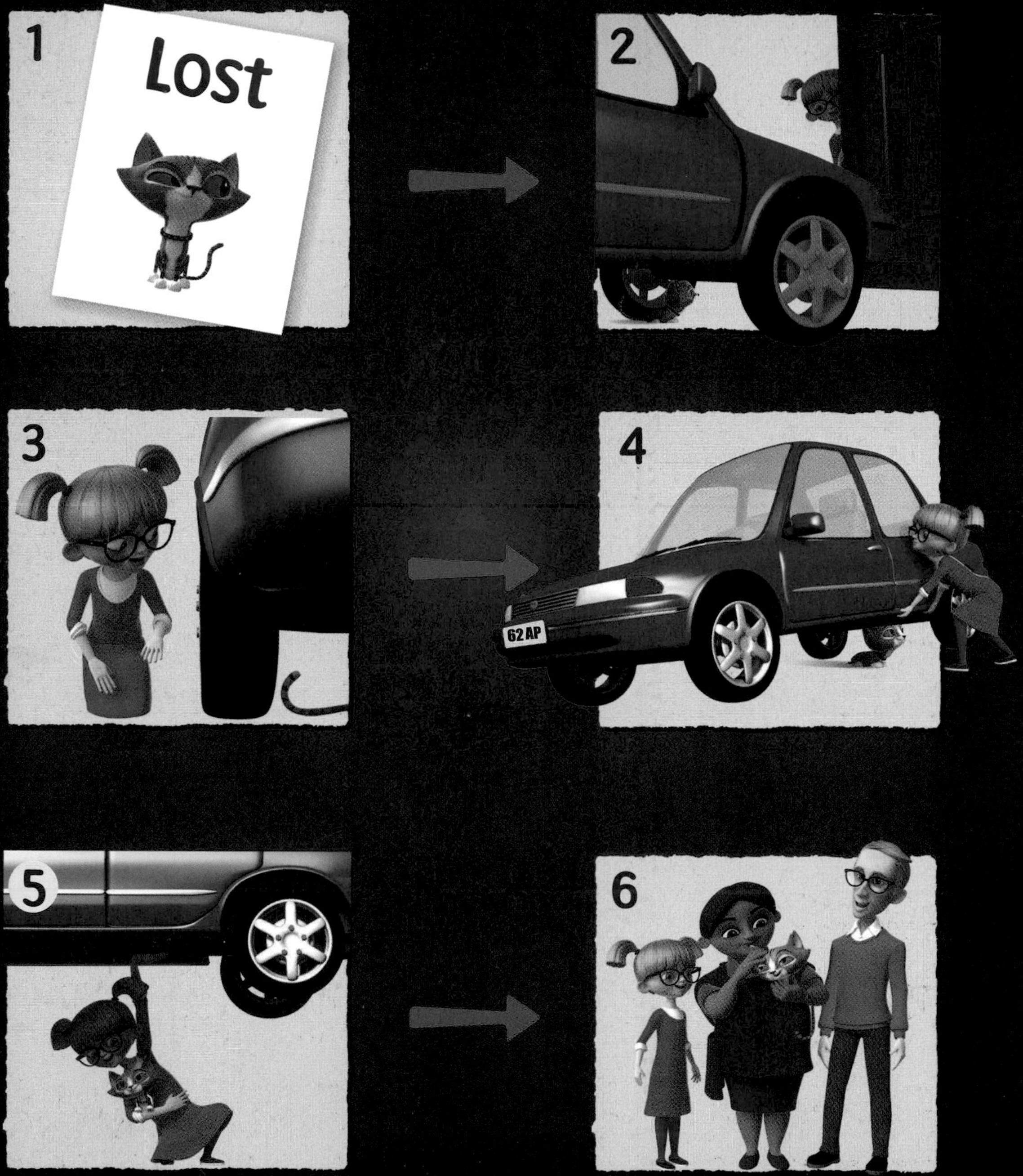